Mantras
To Help Kids Win At Life
Classroom Edition

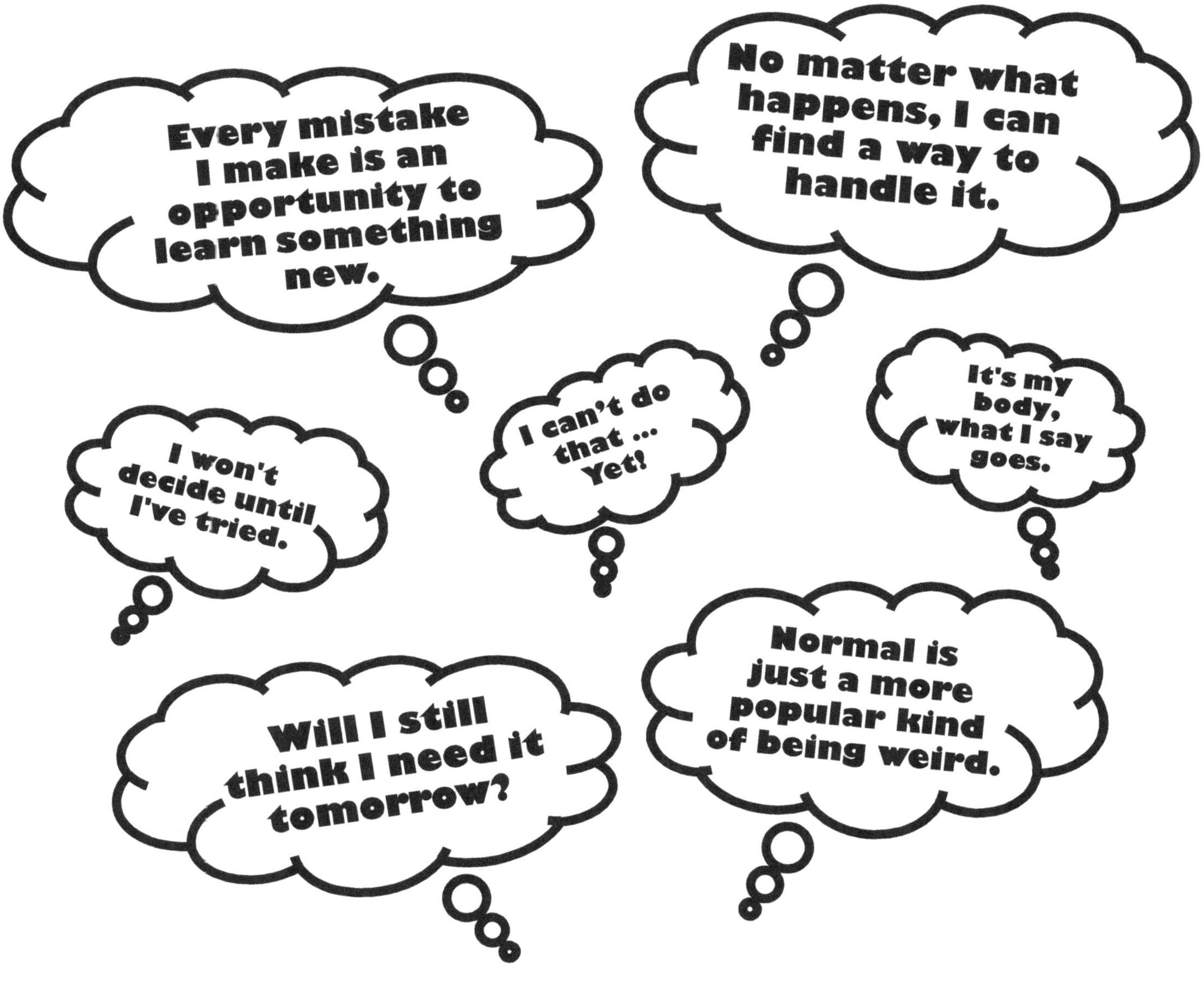

> Every mistake I make is an opportunity to learn something new.

> No matter what happens, I can find a way to handle it.

> I won't decide until I've tried.

> I can't do that ... Yet!

> It's my body, what I say goes.

> Will I still think I need it tomorrow?

> Normal is just a more popular kind of being weird.

Colin M. Drysdale

Pictish Beast Publications

Text Copyright © 2019 Colin M. Drysdale
Imprint and Layout Copyright © 2019 Colin M. Drysdale /Pictish Beast Publications

All rights reserved.
This is the classroom edition of *Mantras To Help Kids Win At Life*. This means that the cost of this book includes the right to photocopy its contents to produce handouts for use in classrooms and for other educational purposes. However, they cannot be reproduced for any 'for-profit' activity without express permission.

ISBN - 978-1-909832-73-2
Published by Pictish Beast Publications, Glasgow, UK.
Published in the United Kingdom
First Printing: 2019. First Edition.

A non-classroom edition of this book for individual children is also available (ISBN: 978-1-909832-72-5).

The cover image is copyright © C.M. Drysdale/Pictish Beast Publications

www.PictishBeastPublications.com

What is a Mantra?

A mantra is a short, easy-to-remember phrase that, if you repeat it to yourself, will help remind you how to positively respond to or cope with a specific situation you may find yourself in. This makes mantras excellent tools for helping children to prepare for, and deal with, anything life has to throw at them. In addition, if children get into the habit of using the right kind of mantras on a regular basis, this will help them build a better brain equipped with some really useful tools that will help them to have a more positive view of life, and that will help them deal with almost any situation they may encounter.

What's in this Workbook?

This is a classroom edition of the *Mantras To Help Kids Win At Life* workbook. It has been specifically designed and formatted to allow teachers to easily create handouts from it for use in primary classrooms. It contains:

- A set of mantras which have been carefully created based on the results of the latest research into human psychology to help children develop a range of important life skills, including a growth mindset, self-control, resilience, persistence and body safety. Together, these mantras form a mental tool kit that can help children achieve more, cope better with adversity, and leave them feeling more relaxed and happier.
- Twelve easy-to-photocopy double-page spreads than can be used to create classroom handouts. Each one features a different mantra and consists of the mantra itself, advice about when it can be used, information about how it helps, ways to practice using it, and an interactive opportunity for your students to try the mantra out. This involves either getting your students to draw a picture of them using it, or completing a short conversation a child might have based on it. This will help your students better understand how and when to use this mantra.
- Information on how to encourage your students to use mantras in their daily lives, and on how you can incorporate the use of mantras into the rest of your teaching. This includes advice on how to help your students create their own mantras.
- A series of blank templates that you can use to encourage your students to come up with their own mantras based on their own experiences and personal circumstances.
- A brief summary of the psychological principles on which these mantras are based, along with information about where you can learn more about them.

Thus, this workbook contains all the information you need to introduce mantras into your classroom, and use them to help your students develop the psychological tools they need to give the best possible chance of growing into happy and successful adults.

How To Use The Contents Of This Workbook In Your Classroom

When it comes to using the contents of this workbook in your classroom, your students will get the most from it if you work though all twelve mantras, one at a time, over a series of several weeks. However, this is not the only way that you can use it. In particular, if you don't have the time to do this, you can select the individual mantras that you feel would be the most useful to them, and work through these as, and when, you see fit.

To work through a mantra, start by photocopying its double-page spread to create a handout for each student in your class. Next, give your students a brief introduction to what mantras are and why they are useful. This can be done using the short paragraph at the bottom of this page. If you have covered this previously, ask your students if they can remember what a mantra is and get them to repeat this definition back to you. Once you have done this, read out the mantra you have selected for a particular session and ask your students to repeat it back to you. Next, explain to them the types of situations where it can be useful to use the mantra, and how it can help, then ask them to suggest specific situations where they could use this particular mantra. After you have done this, you can get your students to practice using it by playing the game or discussing examples of the mantra being used. This can be done as a class or in groups. Finally, ask your students to fill in the interactive exercise that accompanies each mantra. This will consist of either completing a conversation that a child might have based on the mantra, or drawing a picture to illustrate the mantra being used. When these conversations and illustrations have been finished, they can be put on your classroom wall to help remind your students to use the mantras they have learned on a regular basis.

Once you have finished working through some, or all, of these mantras, your students will further benefit from them if you can incorporate their usage into the rest of your teaching. You can find ideas and advice on how to do this towards the end of this workbook.

Mantra Definition For Children

A mantra is a short, easy-to-remember phrase that, if you repeat it to yourself, will help remind you how to positively respond to and cope with a specific situation you may find yourself in. This makes mantras excellent tools for helping you to prepare for, and deal with, anything life has to throw at you. In addition, if you use the right kind of mantras on a regular basis, they will help you build a better brain equipped with some really useful tools that will help you to have a more positive view of life, and that will help you deal with almost any situation you may encounter.

Mantra One

"I can't do that ... Yet!"

When Should I Use It?

Use this mantra whenever you find yourself thinking that you can't do something, or when you've tried to do something new and you didn't manage to do it right away.

How Does It Help?

This mantra reminds you that just because you cannot do something now, it doesn't mean that you'll never be able to do it. In particular, even if you find that you can't do something the first time you try it (or the second, or the third, or even the 100th), if you keep trying, you'll get it eventually. Sometimes you may have to take a break and come back to it later before you finally succeed, but this is okay.

How Can I Practice Using It?

You can practice using this mantra by playing a game with a friend or family member. Take it in turns to ask each other whether you can do something. Make that something as weird, wild and wacky as possible, such as 'Can you juggle with jelly?' or 'Can you put makeup on a monkey?'. No matter what it is, the person being asked the question has to answer 'I can't do that ... Yet!'

Draw a picture of yourself thinking this mantra while faced with something that you don't know how to do. This could be something as ordinary as riding a bicycle or tying your shoelaces for yourself, or something as extraordinary as flying an aeroplane or climbing a massive mountain.

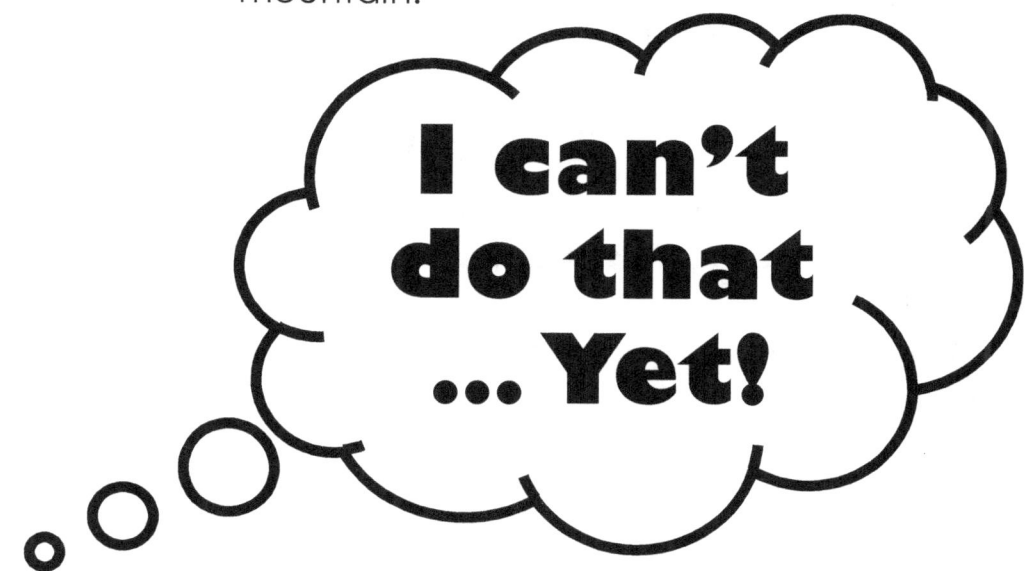

Mantra Two

"Smell the flower ... blow out the candle."

When Should I Use It?

Use this mantra whenever you feel yourself getting worried, nervous, anxious or upset. This mantra isn't meant to be said out loud, rather it is one you say silently to yourself in your head. As you say the first part, breathe in slowly and deeply through your nose as if you're smelling a flower, then hold your breath for a second before breathing out again, just as slowly, through your mouth, as if you're trying to gently blow out a candle while you say the second part.

How Does It Help?

When you are worried, nervous, anxious or upset, your body reacts by entering what is known as a flight-or-fight state. This causes your heart to race and your breathing to become rapid and shallow. Our brains interpret this as meaning that something dangerous is about to happen (even if it's not), and as a result we feel anxious. This mantra works by slowing down your breathing. This, in turn, causes your body to respond by leaving the flight-or-fight state and entering a much more calm and relaxed one. This tells your brain that everything is fine and it is okay for it to relax.

How Can I Practice Using It?

The best way to practice this mantra is to set aside a few minutes at the same time each day, such as when you first wake up in the morning, when you get in from school or just before you go to bed at night. During this time, find yourself a quiet spot (like your bedroom), and turn off any distractions, such as the TV or music. Make yourself as comfortable as possible and then repeat this mantra to yourself in your head while breathing in and out as instructed. Concentrate on your breathing, and see if you can feel the effect it is having on your body. By practicing this mantra on a regular basis, you'll find it becomes much easier to use when you really need it.

Beneath the thought bubble on the left, draw a picture yourself smelling a flower, and then beneath the right hand one, draw a picture of you blowing out a candle.

Mantra Three

"No matter what happens, I can find a way to handle it."

When Should I Use It?

Use this mantra any time you are feeling worried or nervous about what might happen next, whether that's in a few minutes time or years into the future. This mantra is best used in conjunction with mantra two ('*Smell the flower, blow out the candle*').

How Does It Help?

From time to time, everyone worries about what might happen in the future. This is completely normal. However, when they enter your head, these types of worries can sometimes grow and multiply until they squeeze out all other thoughts. When this happens, it can cause you to panic and this can stop you from doing things you might otherwise want to do. Repeating this mantra to yourself not only helps bring these worries back under control, it can also stop them from spreading in the first place. This helps keep your mind clear and free to think about things more rationally. This gives you the mental space to come up with a well-thought out strategy for dealing with the situation you were worrying about. This mantra is especially effective when used with the deep and slow breathing pattern associated with mantra two.

How Can I Practice Using It?

You can practice using this mantra by sitting down with a friend or family member. Take turns in coming up with as wild and bizarre situations as possible, such as '*Could you handle finding a lion under your bed?*' or '*Could you handle being asked to sing for the Queen?*'. No matter what the situation you are presented with, you always reply '*No matter what happens, I can find a way to handle it.*' The person presenting the situation then asks '*How?*', and you then have to come up with a strategy of how you would deal with it.

Think of a really weird situation that you imagine you might find difficult to handle, and then draw a picture of yourself saying this mantra when you are faced with it.

> **No matter what happens, I can find a way to handle it!**

Mantra Four

"It's my body, what I say goes."

When Should I Use It?

Use this mantra when you feel that someone, whether they are another child or an adult, is invading your personal space or is trying to make you do something that makes you feel uncomfortable.

How Does It Help?

We all have an invisible bubble around us that defines our personal space. This mantra reminds you that each of us has the right to say who is allowed to enter this personal space, and who is not. It also reminds you that you have the right to say no if someone tries to enter your personal space without asking you first or getting your permission. This applies to everyone, regardless of whether they are kids or adults, friends, strangers or even relatives.

How Can I Practice Using It?

You can practice using this mantra by playing a simple game with a friend or family member. One person starts off as the body-borrower, and they ask the other person if they can borrow a part of their body (like a nose, or an ear, or a little toe). The other person tells them no. The would-be borrower then asks why, and the other person replies (in a loud voice): 'It's my body, what I say goes!'

Think of a part of your body a body-borrower might want to borrow and write it in the first speech bubble. Once you have done this, practice using this mantra to respond to their request.

Mantra Five

"Will I still think I need it tomorrow?"

When Should I Use It?

Use this mantra when you find yourself thinking that you really, really must have something, such as a particular toy, computer game or to go to a specific event.

How Does It Help?

Our brains are wired in such a way that when we first encounter something new, we see it as incredibly desirable and we instantly want it. This feeling can, and often does, temporarily hijack our brains, driving out other, more rational thoughts. The more we give in to such instant cravings, the more intensely our brains respond in this manner, and the more difficult it becomes to control them. However, these sudden cravings are a very transient brain state, and often if we wait a little while, our brains calm down, and we can start to see that we don't really need whatever it was that initially seemed so desirable. This mantra encourages you to think about how you will view an item once your brain has returned to this calmer, more rational state. Doing this will help you to control these sudden cravings.

How Can I Practice Using It?

You can practice this mantra whenever you find yourself feeling that you really, really want something. Repeat this mantra to yourself and then make yourself wait at least a day before you do anything about your sudden want. After a day, think about the item again, and see whether you still really want it. The more often you do this, the more often you'll find that if you wait before giving in to sudden desires, they will simply evaporate.

Draw a picture of yourself looking in a shop window filled with things that you might like, but that you don't really need, and thinking of this mantra.

Mantra Six

"If I look for it, I can always find something in every day that made me happy."

When Should I Use It?

Use this mantra at the end of any day when you are feeling unhappy, when nothing seems to be going right for you, when you feel the whole world is against you, or when something bad has happened in your life.

How Does It Help?

When we are unhappy or when something bad happens in our lives, it is only natural to dwell on it. However, when we focus too much on our unhappiness or the bad things that have happened to us, and nothing else, it creates a feedback loop in our brains which makes us feel even worse. This is known as rumination, and it makes it very difficult for us to see any good in our lives. This mantra helps to remind you that no matter how bad things are, there are still good things out there too, and even on the worst of days, there will always have been something that has made you feel happy, even if it was only for a few seconds. By focusing on these good things, rather than the bad ones, it can stop your brain from becoming trapped in a state of rumination. This, in turn, allows you to focus on changing your life for the better, rather than getting stuck on focusing on the things that make you unhappy.

How Can I Practice Using It?

You can practice this mantra by doing an exercise called 'Three Happy Things'. To do this exercise, sit down with a friend or family member and tell them three things about your day that made you happy. If you don't have anyone to sit down with (or if you don't want to do this), this is okay and you can write them down instead. You can also just do it in your head as you lie in bed at the end of the day before going to sleep. The more frequently you do this exercise the better, and it will have the biggest positive impact on your life if you get into the habit of doing it at least once a day.

At the end of a day, find yourself somewhere quiet and think back over everything you did, saw or that happened in it, and see if you can come up with three things that made you really happy, even if it was just for a moment. It could be something really simple like the sound of your little brother laughing or a dog licking your face, or something really big like being able to swim across the swimming pool without armbands for the very first time. Once you have thought of your three happy things, write them in the speech bubbles below.

From *Mantras To Help Kids Win At Life* by Colin M. Drysdale

Mantra Seven

"I will try hard, be kind and think before I do."

When Should I Use It?

Use this mantra at the start of each day, when you're going through the school gate, or just before you try anything new.

How Does It Help?

This mantra reminds you of three important things that are good habits to get into. These are trying as hard as you possibly can, being kind to yourself and to those around you, and thinking through the potential consequences of your actions before you do anything to ensure that they are appropriate for the situation that you are in. By reminding yourself of these habits on a regular basis, you are more likely to practice them, and the more you practice them, the more they will become an automatic part of your everyday life. This will help you develop what is called a growth mindset, which is a way of viewing the world that is likely to lead to you being much happier and successful in whatever you choose to do with your life.

How Can I Practice Using It?

The best way to practice this mantra is to sit down with a friend or family member and take it in turns to come up with examples of people displaying one or more of these habits. These examples can come from your own life, from the lives of your friends and family, from books you have read, TV shows you've watched or films you have seen. For each example you come up with, see if you can explain how using the habit benefitted the person either in the short or the longer term.

Draw picture of yourself leaving your house first thing in the morning, making sure that the thought bubbles for this mantra are coming out of you head.

Mantra Eight

"I won't decide until I've tried."

When Should I Use It?

Use this mantra whenever you find yourself confronted with a new or unfamiliar place, activity or situation. This might be starting at a new school, trying a new sport, going to a club for the first time, or eating something new.

How Does It Help?

It is completely normal to worry about new or unfamiliar situations. However, these worries can easily get out of hand and stop us doing things that we otherwise might wish to do. This can lead to our lives becoming very closed off from the new experiences and opportunities that allow us to grow as people. It's amazing how often something we were certain we would never, ever like, turns out to be really enjoyable once we give it a go. This mantra reminds you that you cannot let a fear of the unfamiliar stop you trying new things. After all, the worst thing that can happen when you try something new is that you find that you don't like it. In that case, you don't have to do it again. However, if you don't try it, you will never know if you'd have liked it or not, and this can lead you to missing out on some amazing opportunities. When you look back on your life, it will be the opportunities you didn't take that you'll regret more than the ones you took, even if it turned out that you didn't like doing a particular thing.

How Can I Practice Using It?

You can practice using this mantra by sitting down with a friend or family member and taking turns to ask each other if you'd like to do all sorts of weird things, like eating a worm sandwich, or drinking a slug milkshake. No matter what is asked, the other person replies, *'I won't decide until I've tried'*. The stranger the things are that you ask if a person would like to do, the funnier the game will become.

From Mantras To Help Kids Win At Life by Colin M. Drysdale – Page 15

Think about something really, really wild and wacky that you've never done before, and that you imagine might not be particularly pleasant to do. Write it into the top speech bubble. Once you have done this, practice giving this mantra in response to being asked if you'd like to do it.

Mantra Nine

"Every mistake I make is an opportunity to learn something new."

When Should I Use It?

Use this mantra whenever you find yourself feeling bad because you made a mistake, or whenever you find yourself worrying that you might make one, especially if it's stopping you trying your best to do something.

How Does It Help?

Everyone makes mistakes, and making mistakes is one of the best ways of learning how to do something new. However, if we worry too much about making mistakes, or if we find ourselves feeling bad because we made one, we can end up not trying new things, and not pushing ourselves to reach our full potential. This is not to say that some mistakes are not bad, or that they might not have big consequences, but if we do our very best to learn something from every mistake we make, then we are much less likely to make the same mistake again. This mantra helps you change the way you think about the mistakes you make and see them not as bad things that must be avoided at all costs, but as part of the normal learning process. It also reminds you to make sure that you do learn from them.

How Can I Practice Using It?

You can practice using this mantra by sitting down with a friend or family member. Take it in turn to come up with a silly situation, and an amusing mistake you could make in it. The other person then has to respond by saying *'Every mistake I make is an opportunity to learn something new'*, and then they must come up with a suggestion for something new they could learn from making that specific mistake.

Draw a picture of yourself making a really silly mistake, like accidently wearing your slippers to school, and then using this mantra to remind yourself that it is an opportunity to learn something new. What could you learn from accidently wearing your slippers to school?

Every mistake I make is an opportunity to learn something new!

Mantra Ten

"I measure my success against my past self, and not just against the achievements of others."

When Should I Use It?

Use this mantra whenever you find yourself comparing yourself to others when you are trying to learn something new, or improve your ability to do anything, whether at school, on the sports field or at home. This mantra is particularly useful when you are learning in a group environment.

How Does It Help?

It is always very tempting to compare yourself to those around you in order to see how well you are doing. However, this can make you feel bad if you feel you are not doing as well as everyone else. This mantra reminds you that the best person to compare yourself to, in order to see how well you are doing is your past self as this allows you to see how far you've come. For example, if you are in a class learning to juggle, and if after a month everyone else can juggle four balls while you can only juggle three, you may feel disheartened if you only compare yourself to those around you. However, if you also compare yourself to how you were a month ago (when you couldn't juggle at all), you'll be able to see that you can now juggle much better than before. This is much more rewarding and will help encourage you to keep going until you, too, can juggle four balls at once.

How Can I Practice Using It?

The best way to practice this mantra is to think of a situation where you regularly find yourself comparing your success to those around you rather than to your past self. This might be when you get the results of your homework back, when you have a test at school, when practising sports, or when playing with your friends. Once you have identified such a situation, set yourself the target of repeating this mantra to yourself every time you find yourself in it from now on. This will help the ideas behind it become an automatic part of your way of thinking about measuring your achievements.

From *Mantras To Help Kids Win At Life* by Colin M. Drysdale

On the left hand side of this page, draw a picture of yourself as a little baby, and then draw a picture of yourself today on the right hand side. Think about three things you can do now that you couldn't do when you were younger and write them in the thought bubbles.

Mantra Eleven

"I can't control the actions of others, but I can control how I respond to them."

When Should I Use It?

Use this mantra whenever you find yourself feeling frustrated, angry or hurt by the behaviour of others, regardless of whether they are friends, classmates, family members, or even strangers that you don't know.

How Does It Help?

This mantra reminds you of two important things. Firstly, no matter how much you may wish you could, you cannot control how other people behave, and trying to do so will just leave you feeling angry and frustrated. Secondly, what you can control is how you respond to their actions. If you can remain calm and in control when someone else is trying to annoy you or wind you up, you'll not only feel better about it (because you have remained in control), you will also often find that they stop doing it because they are not getting the response they were looking for. This works particularly well in situations where someone is trying to bully you. However, it also works in situations where someone's unthinking actions impact you accidentally rather than on purpose. The aim here is not to change how the other persons actions make you feel (such as feeling frustrated, angry or hurt) as these are often valid feelings, but only how you respond so that you remain in control of your actions rather than lashing out at those around you.

How Can I Practice Using It?

You can practice this mantra by sitting down with a friend or family member. Take turns in suggesting the actions of others that might frustrate, anger or hurt you. Respond by saying '*I can't control the actions of others, but I can control how I respond.*' The other person then asks '*How would you respond?*', and you then need to come up with a way to respond to that situation which would reflect how the situation would make you feel, but that wouldn't result in you losing control as a result of these feelings.

From *Mantras To Help Kids Win At Life* by Colin M. Drysdale

Think of an action that someone else might do that you'd find really frustrating and write this in the top speech bubble. Now think of a way you could respond which would reflect how the situation would make you feel, but that wouldn't result in you losing control as a result of these feelings. Write this response in the speech bubble at the bottom of the page.

Mantra Twelve

"Normal is just a more popular kind of being weird."

When Should I Use It?
Use this mantra whenever you find yourself thinking that you are weird or that you don't fit in with those around you.

How Does It Help?
This mantra reminds you that there is no such thing as being normal, that everyone is an individual, and that, when you think about it, everyone is weird in some way or other. The important thing is that you need to be your own kind of weird, and not the kind of weird you think someone else thinks you should be just because they call it normal. After all, it's better to be your own kind of weird and happy, than to pretend to be something you're not, as this can leave you feeling very unhappy.

How Can I Practice Using It?
The best way to practice this mantra is to play a game with a friend or family member. One of you starts by saying 'Normal people ...' before completing the sentence with something they consider normal (for example 'Normal people like watching football'). The other then replies, 'But that's weird because ...' and completes the sentence with a reason why this thing that other people might consider normal is, when you stop and think about it, actually a bit weird. In the example above, about watching football, you might respond by saying 'But that's weird because all they're doing is watching a bunch of people who get paid a lot of money chase a small ball around a large field.'

Draw a picture of yourself saying this mantra as you do something that you think is normal, but draw yourself wearing clothes that people wouldn't usually wear for doing it. This could be wearing a fairy princess costume to play football, wearing your best clothes to go swimming, or wearing your pyjamas to school!

Incorporating The Use Of Mantras Into The Rest Of Your Teaching

The mantras in this book are most useful when they become a part of your students' everyday lives. This means that they will have a greater impact on your students if you can incorporate the use of mantras into the rest of your teaching and your wider classroom life. There are many different ways you can do this, but at all times make sure that you do it in a non-judgemental and constructive manner. In particular, don't try to force your students to adopt them, and resist the urge to instantly leap in and correct them if you feel that they are using them inappropriately. Instead, give them the opportunity, and the time, to work this out for themselves, and if they don't, try to lead them gently towards this realisation. This is because the more they feel that working with mantras comes from themselves, rather than being forced on them by you, their teacher, the more they will benefit from them, both now, and for the rest of their lives. Ways that you can incorporate the use of these mantras into the rest of your teaching include:

1. Once you have introduced your students to any of the mantras from this workbook, encourage your students to start using them whenever they find themselves in a relevant situation. For example, you may find a student saying that they just can't do something. In this instance, you can remind them to say *'I can't do it ...Yet'* rather than just *'I can't do it'*. Similarly, if you find you have students who are being overly critical about how well they are doing, you can remind them of mantra ten (*'I measure my success against my past self, and not just against the achievements of others'*) and then remind them of how much they have improved at whatever they are doing since the start of the term. The same applies to whenever your students make a mistake (remind them of mantra nine) or when they get frustrated or angry at the actions of others (remind them of mantra eleven). In all such instances, rather than simply repeating the relevant mantra to the student, encourage them to recall and recite it for themselves. This will not only help demonstrate how they can use the mantras, it will also help reinforce the neural pathways where the information is stored, making it more likely that they will start using the mantra when they find themselves in a relevant situation.

2. You can help your students remember the mantras from this workbook by creating a *Wall of Mantras* in your classroom and illustrate it with the pictures and conversations which your students have completed as part of learning about the individual mantras. This will act as a gentle, but continual, reminder for your students to remind them to use the mantras whenever they encounter a relevant situation.

3. You can also encourage your students to come up with their own mantras whenever they encounter a tricky situation in class. This is particularly powerful because it teaches them to learn how to build their own mantras to encapsulate lessons they learn from their own lives. However, while your students may well be good at coming up with general ideas for new mantras, you may need to help them with the exact wording to make sure they are as effective as possible. Advice on how to do this is provided later in this workbook, along with some blank templates for writing out the mantras and creating worksheets based on them. Whenever your students create a new manta, you can add it to your *Wall of Mantras*.

4. You can also use positive praise and highlighting to encourage your students to use mantras. This is most effective if you do it whenever you see one of your students using a mantra in an appropriate situation. By highlighting the situation, you let the student know both that they have been seen, and that you appreciate the effort they put in to using the mantra appropriately. When doing this, make sure that you clearly spell out exactly to the student what you saw and why you are praising them for it. This ensures that they understand what they did well, and so feel encouraged to do it again in the future. You can find more information about how best to give positive praise at *howtoraiseahappygenius.com/parental-skill-seven-ways-to-positively-praise-your-child/*.

5. When highlighting the spontaneous use of mantras, it is often useful to introduce *You've Been Seen* cards specific to using the mantras provided in this workbook or mantras which you have developed in your own classroom. Depending on how you operate within your particular school, these can be traded for rewards, exchanged for ranking points or simply operate as their own rewards on charts showing who has been seen using mantras correctly.

6. You can also encourage the appropriate use of mantras by priming. Priming involves reminding your students about a specific mantra before they enter a relevant situation. This helps them understand when individual mantras can be used to help them deal with specific situations, The most effective way to do this is to explain to your students what they are about to do, and then ask them what mantras they think might be relevant to the situation they are about to encounter. Asking them to actively recall and recite the mantras for themselves (rather than just telling them what mantra to use) reinforces the neural pathways to where this information is stored in their brains and this will increase the likelihood that they will become a normal part of their thinking. This can be further enhanced by asking them to explain why they think the mantra they came up with is relevant to the situation they are about to encounter. Remember, however, not to be critical if you feel their choice is inappropriate as this can discourage them from trying to use mantras for themselves. Instead, praise them for being able to recall the mantra they brought up and ask them if they can think of another, more relevant one.

7. After you have introduced your students to a new mantra (or they have created a new one for themselves), you can ask them whether they have used the mantra, or whether they have been in situations where they could have used it to help them deal with it. This acts as a reminder not just to remember the mantras but to actually use them. This is best done a week or so after a mantra has first been learned. However, it will have the greatest benefit if the students know they are going to be asked about this as this will encourage them to make more of an effort to actually use it.

8. You can also have classroom discussions about whether characters in any books your students are reading could have benefitted from using individual mantras, what situations they could have used them in and how this might have changed the outcome of the story if they had. This will help your students see how using mantras can change an individual's life for the better, and encourage your students to use them in their daily lives.

Phrasing To Use And To Avoid When Creating Your Own Mantras

The exact phrasing used for a mantra can have a big impact on its effectiveness in helping your students expand and develop their mental tool kit. This may, at first, make working with your students to come up with new mantras that are specific to situations they may encounter seem a little daunting, there are a few simple rules to follow that will go a long way to helping you to create the best possible mantras to help your students cope with any given situation. These rules are:

1. It is better if mantras are worded in the first person (me or I) rather than the second person (you) or the third person (he/she/people). This will encourage your child to embrace the mantra and the message it contains.

2. Avoid the use of words like Should/Shouldn't, and Must/Mustn't. This is because these words can make children feel like they are doing something because they are being told to, rather than that they are doing it off their own volition and for their own benefit. Instead, use words like Will or Won't, as these encourage children to take ownership of the mantra.

3. Try to make sure that all mantras are worded in such a way that they focus on encouraging positive actions rather than preventing negatives ones. This is because children tend to focus on the types of actions they hear the most about, and this means that positive mantras encourage positive behaviours, while negative ones risk focusing too much attention on negative behaviours.

4. Make sure that mantras are worded in such a way that they focus on behaviours and responses, rather than on the fundamental characteristics of who your students are. This is because mantras that focus on what your students perceives to be unalterable characteristics can have a negative effect on them if they fail to live up to them. For example, when trying to encourage a you students to think about the impact of their actions on others, simply getting them to say '*I am a kind person*' will set them up for failure as there are always times when, for whatever reason, they will find themselves acting in an unkind way. In contrast, if they use the mantra '*be kind*', this reinforces that they should try to act in a kind and considerate manner, but it doesn't set them up for failure if there are occasions when they find themselves not being as kind as they could be to themselves or to those around them.

5. Try to make sure that any mantras your students comes up with do not result in them prioritising the well-being of others over their own well-being. For example, the mantra '*I shouldn't hurt the feelings of others*' will likely encourage your students to avoid hurting others at all costs, even if it is detrimental to their own well-being, and this is not a positive outcome. In contrast, '*I will try to be considerate of the feelings of others*' has the same general meaning, but it allows for situations where your students need to put their own feelings above those of others, if that is what is best in a specific instance.

Mantra

When Should I Use It?

How Does It Help?

How Can I Practice Using it?

From *Mantras To Help Kids Win At Life* by Colin M. Drysdale – Page 32

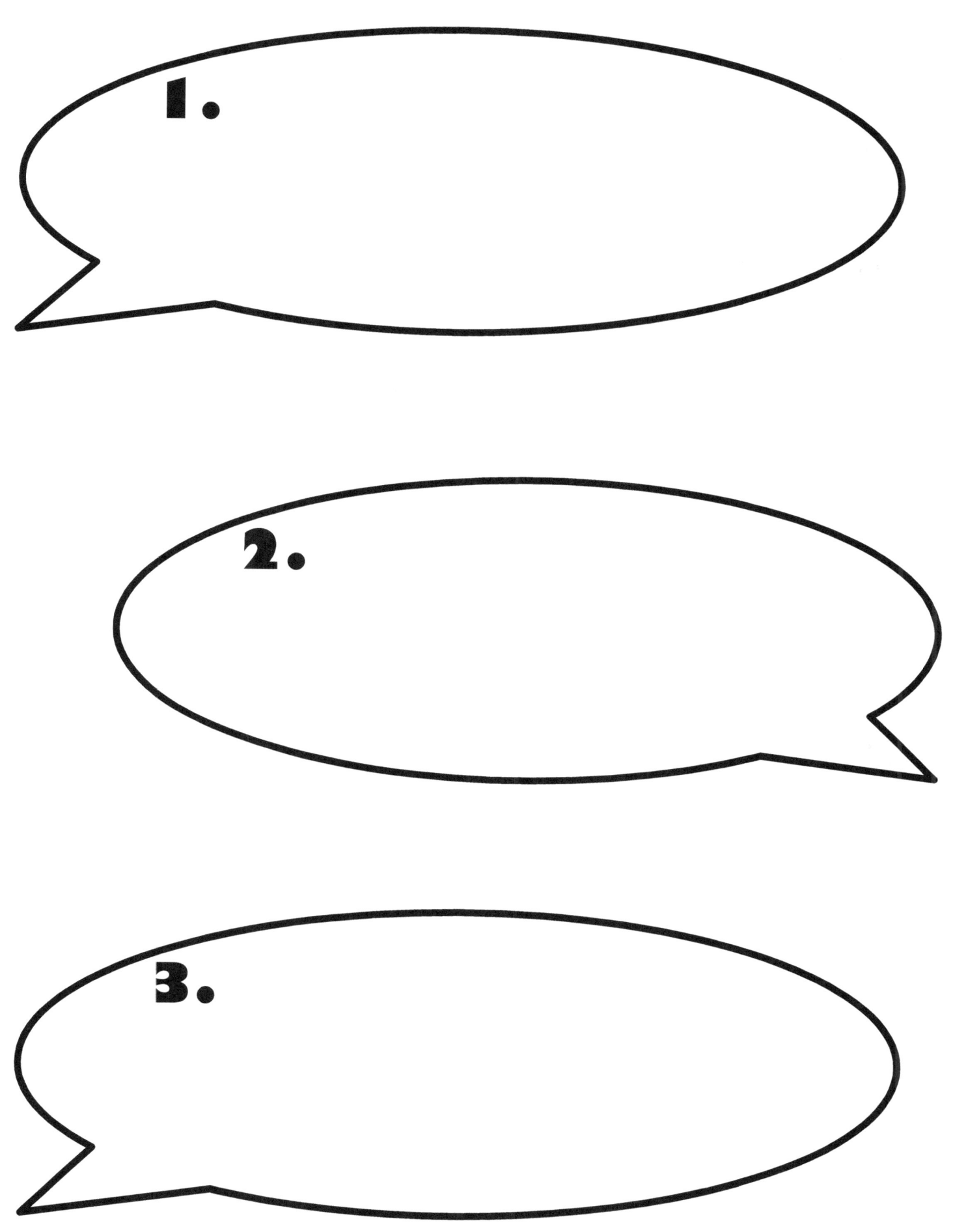

From *Mantras To Help Kids Win At Life* by Colin M. Drysdale – Page 34

The Science Behind Using These Mantras In Everyday Life

The mantras in this workbook have been created using a range of psychological principles with the aim of helping parents and children apply them to their child's life in a simple and straight forward manner. Foremost amongst these are five inter-related elements. These are growth mindset theory, cognitive behaviour therapy, the chimp mind management model, nudge theory, and wise psychological interventions.

1. **Growth Mindset Theory:** Growth mindset theory is the idea that the way we perceive problems we encounter is a more important factor in determining whether we will solve them than any innate abilities. In short, if we believe that we are capable of solving a problem by working hard at it, we are much more likely to be able to do so than if we believe that the ability to solve any particular problem is down to some sort of innate talent that we were born with. Building on this basic tenet, the mantras in this workbook aim to encourage children to see their abilities not as something that were fixed at birth, but as something that they can develop over time, and that it is within their power to choose how these abilities develop. If you wish to learn more about growth mindset theory, you can read *Mindset: How You Can Fulfil Your Potential* by Carol Dweck.

2. **Cognitive Behavioural Therapy (CBT):** Cognitive behavioural therapy, or CBT for short, is an approach which encourages people to deal with problems they face by changing the way that they think about them, and so how they respond to them. While CBT requires a level of self-awareness and self-examination that most children simply do not have, the mantras in this workbook encourage children to respond to specific situations in a psychologically positive manner that will provide a firm foundation for their future psychological development. This, in turn, encourages them to look at any issues they may encounter in their lives in such a way that they feel they have the mental tools to work out how best to respond to them. If you wish to learn more about cognitive behavioural therapy, you can read *Change Your Thinking: Positive and Practical Ways To Overcome Stress, Negative Emotions and Self-defeating Behaviour Using CBT* by Sarah Edelman.

3. **Chimp Mind Management Model:** The chimp mind management model was developed by Professor Steve Peters as a way to help people understand how their brains work, and how they can program them to react in a conscious, positive and logical manner rather than in the instinctive, emotional manner that is the default within the human brain. One of the best ways to do this is to provide pre-considered routines of how to react to different situations. This, then, provides a set of mental tools that we can use to help us deal with the challenges we face in our everyday lives. While relatively simple, the mantras in this workbook have been specifically created to provide children with tools that they can apply to situations they are likely to encounter in their daily lives, both as children and as adults. These include things like making mistakes, running into difficulties in completing a specific task, and self-confidence. Thus, taken as a whole, the mantras in this workbook provide a tool set that helps children deal with all that life may throw at them in a positive, conscious and logical manner. If you wish to learn more about the chimp mind management model, you can read *The Chimp Paradox: The Mind Management Programme To Help You Achieve Success, Confidence and Happiness* by Professor Steve Peters.

4. **Nudge Theory:** Nudge theory is the idea that, if chosen carefully, relatively small changes in the way that information is presented to a person can have large positive impacts on their actions. For this workbook, this means that the wording of the mantras included in it have been specifically chosen to give the highest likelihood that the positive message behind them will be understood by children and will be incorporated into their own personal set of mind management tools. This gives the greatest chance that these tool will be available when they are needed. If you wish to learn more about nudge theory, you can read *Nudge: Improving Decisions about Health, Wealth, and Happiness* by Cass Sunstein and Richard Thaler.

5. **Wise Psychological Interventions (WPIs):** WPIs are a relatively new area of psychology, but the principle behind them is very straight forward and can be thought of as building on nudge theory. WPI theory states that is it not enough to simply provide a person with a useful piece of information that will benefit them, it also has to be presented to them at just the right time in order to have the biggest possible positive impact. In fact, WPI research suggests that the right thing presented to a person in the right way at just the right time can have large, and long-lasting, positive impacts upon them and their psychology. Each mantra in this workbook has been designed to be just the right thing presented in just the right way to help children develop a positive mental tool for use in a specific circumstance that they are likely to encounter in their everyday life. However, the trouble with applying WPI theory to child development is that it can be very difficult to identify when an individual child will most benefit from receiving a specific piece of advice or information, especially when it comes in the form of a psychological tool. This issue has been dealt with for the mantras in this workbook by providing advice on how best to practice them. If the mantras are practised regularly, this will mean that they will already be available to the child at the moment when they have the potential to have the biggest impact upon them and their psychological development. If you wish to learn more about wise psychological interventions, you can read this article from *New Scientist* magazine: *https://www.newscientist.com/article/2080024-wise-interventions-when-your-brain-needs-a-stronger-nudge/*.

www.ingramcontent.com/pod-product-compliance
Lightning Source LLC
Chambersburg PA
CBHW050716090526
44587CB00019B/3404